Bird Eggs

Raven

Gyrfalcon

Red-throated Loon

Long-tailed Duck

Snow Bunting

Snowy Owl

Rock Ptarmigan

Red Phalarope

Common Eider

Tundra Swan

Thick-billed Murre

Arctic Tern

A Children's Guide to Arctic BIRDS

BY MIA PELLETIER • ILLUSTRATED BY DANNY CHRISTOPHER

FOR THE FUTURE STEWARDS OF THIS WILD AND FARAWAY PLACE.

PUBLISHED BY INHABIT MEDIA INC.
www.inhabitmedia.com

Inhabit Media Inc. (Iqaluit), P.O. Box 11125, Iqaluit, Nunavut, X0A 1H0
(Toronto), 146A Orchard View Blvd., Toronto, Ontario, M4R 1C3

Design and layout copyright © 2014 Inhabit Media Inc.
Text copyright © 2014 Mia Pelletier
Illustrations by Danny Christopher copyright © 2014 Inhabit Media Inc.

Editors: Neil Christopher and Kelly Ward
Designer: Danny Christopher

We acknowledge the financial support of the Government of Canada through the Department of Canadian Heritage Canada Book Fund.

We acknowledge the support of the Canada Council for the Arts for our publishing program.

Printed in Canada

Library and Archives Canada Cataloguing in Publication

Pelletier, Mia, author
    A children's guide to Arctic birds / by Mia Pelletier ; illustrated by
Danny Christopher.

ISBN 978-1-927095-67-6 (bound)

    1. Birds--Canada, Northern--Identification--Juvenile literature.
2. Birds--Canada, Northern--Pictorial works--Juvenile literature.
I. Christopher, Danny, illustrator II. Title. III. Title: Guide to Arctic
birds. IV. Title: Arctic birds.

QL695.P44 2014   j598.09719   C2014-903379-6

Table of Contents

LONG-TAILED DUCK (SUMMER)

Introduction

As spring arrives in the Arctic, the sky hums with beating wings. From the faraway shores of Africa, South America, and Europe, birds wing their way North from all over the world. *But why do they come so far?* The Arctic summer is rich with food, and birds arrive in the millions to fill their bellies and raise their young. The air buzzes with insects, the ocean leaps with fish, wet places on the tundra swarm with tiny larvae, and fresh green plants reach for the sun. The Arctic sun shines both day and night, and birds can hunt for food around the clock. Their chicks must grow quickly, and gather strength for the long journey south before the snow flies again.

For Arctic animals like foxes, ravens, and weasels, who have just survived a long, cold winter, this rush of life to the Arctic provides its own welcome feast. To keep themselves, their eggs, and their chicks safe from hungry predators, birds must have many different ways to hide.

How would you hide something in a land without trees? You could hide *yourself* by putting on camouflage clothes and crouching very quietly in the grass—some birds have feathers that are coloured and patterned to help them disappear like this! You could hide an object by getting up on your tip-toes and putting it way up out of reach—some birds keep their eggs safe by laying them high up on the sides of cliffs. You could also tuck something away in a secret place among stones or in a tangle of summer grass—some birds build their nests in spots like these where they are very hard to find. Or, you could cover something up with camouflage paint so that it looks exactly like a bunch of rocks—shorebird eggs are painted like this so that they disappear on the tundra!

By learning where birds nest, what they eat, and how they call, we learn to open our eyes and pay attention to the little things in nature. When we follow the flash of a bird's wing across the tundra, or part the grass at a pond's edge to see a loon sitting quietly on her nest, we forget ourselves for a moment, and remember our place among the wildness of things.

Bird Measurements

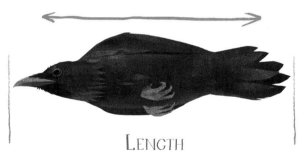

Length
The measurement of a bird from the tip of the beak to the farthest tail feather.

Wingspan
The measurement of a bird from wingtip to wingtip.

 ### Year-round Arctic Birds
When this snowflake appears at the top of a page, it symbolizes the fact that this particular bird can remain in the Arctic all year long.

 ### Migratory Arctic Birds
When this icon appears at the top of a page, it symbolizes the fact that this particular bird migrates to the Arctic. That means that it spends the winter elsewhere and travels to the Arctic to nest in the summer.

 Birds with this symbol stay in some parts of the Arctic all year long, though some populations travel farther south for the winter.

Red Phalarope

Raven

Rock Ptarmigan

Tundra Swan

Gyrfalcon

Snow Bunting

Arctic Tern

Snowy Owl

Long-tailed Duck

Thick-billed Murre

Common Eider

Red-throated Loon

Bird Size Comparison

The silhouette of each bird is represented in scale to give you an idea
of how big these birds are in relation to one another.

Feathers, Bills, and Feet

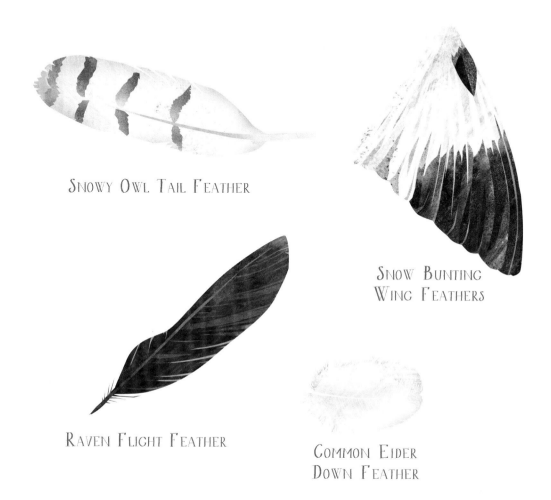

SNOWY OWL TAIL FEATHER

SNOW BUNTING
WING FEATHERS

RAVEN FLIGHT FEATHER

COMMON EIDER
DOWN FEATHER

FEATHERS

What is special about birds? Many other animals have wings, such as butterflies, bats, and bees. Other animals, like turtles, lizards, and frogs, lay eggs. But birds are the *only* animals on earth that are covered in feathers. Feathers keep birds warm and dry, and they allow them to escape their enemies and fly far away as the seasons change. They also help them find and attract mates.

The colours and patterns of a bird's feathers can be changed with the seasons to keep birds safely hidden. Birds change their feathers by moulting. This means that old, worn feathers are shed away and fresh new ones grow in.

RAVEN

TUNDRA SWAN

SNOW BUNTING

FEATHERED FACT: A beak or a bill?
The words "beak" and "bill" are both used for birds. Other animals, such as octopuses or turtles, also have beaks, but the word "bill" is most often used for birds. A broad, strong, short bill used for tearing or striking prey, such as those found on owls or hawks, is usually called a "beak."

GYRFALCON

RED-THROATED LOON

BILLS

Bills come in many shapes and sizes. The shape of a bird's bill can tell us a lot about what it eats. Seed-eaters, insect-eaters, and fish-catchers all have uniquely shaped bills. These special shapes help them catch their favourite foods. A long, curved bill is perfect for probing in the mud for tiny animals, while a strong, heavy bill can be handy for breaking seeds. Can you guess what each of these birds might eat by the shape of its bill?

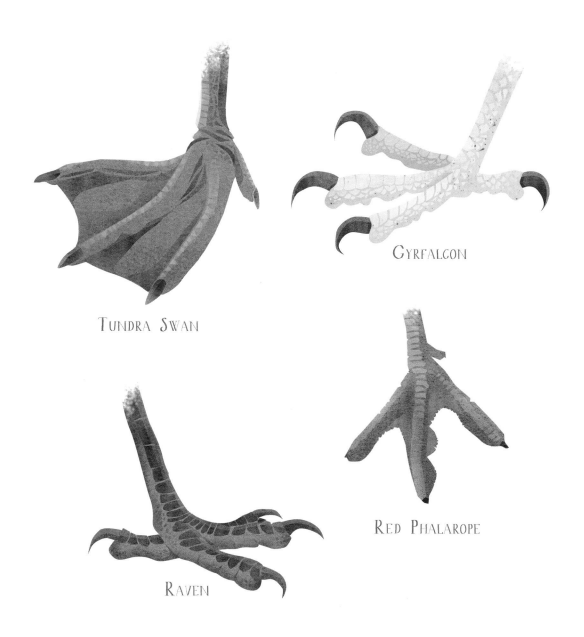

TUNDRA SWAN

GYRFALCON

RED PHALAROPE

RAVEN

FEET

You can also learn a lot about how a bird gets its food by looking at its feet. Some birds, like owls, are hunters. They have strong feet with sharp talons for swooping down and grabbing prey. Other birds are waders, with wide, "lobed" toes that act like floats for walking on wet ground as they feed. Webbed feet are for swimmers and divers, so they can paddle across lakes or use them like flippers to help them race underwater to catch fish.

ARCTIC BIRDS

THICK-BILLED MURRE
INUKTITUT NAME: *AKPA*

↑ LENGTH: 36–48 cm
↓ WINGSPAN: 76 cm

This finely dressed seabird is entirely black and white, and looks like it is wearing a dark, hooded cape. It has black, webbed feet and a thick, dark bill with a fine white stripe. Its wings seem small for its chubby body, and murres must beat their wings very fast in order to fly. The male and female look alike, but differ in the size of their bills.

WHERE TO LOOK: Murres nest in big, noisy colonies on the steep sides of ocean cliffs, high out of reach for most foxes and bears, but not for hungry gulls. Look for the bright lichen that paints the rocks beneath the nest cliffs a brilliant orange colour.

WHAT THEY EAT: Murres will fly long distances from their colony to find good fishing spots. At sea, they are excellent deep-water fliers. They use their wings to race underwater in pursuit of fish and krill, and can dive down to 200 metres below the surface!

LISTEN FOR: Murres make a chorus of roaring *"Aaoorrr! Aaoorr!"* cries that can be heard as you pass by their sea-cliff colonies.

NEST: Murres do not build nests. A single egg is laid on the rocky ledge of a high sea cliff. Each murre likes to lay its egg in the same spot on the cliff ledge, year after year.

EGG: A murre lays 1 large turquoise, cream, or olive-coloured egg covered with brown speckles and squiggles. Murre eggs are pointed on one end and round on the other, so that they roll in a circle and not off the cliff ledge. The parents take turns keeping the egg warm, though the male usually takes the night shift.

CHICK: The downy, brown chick hatches after 30 to 35 days. When it is one-quarter the size of an adult murre, the chick leaps from the cliff to the ocean below and starts swimming south with the male parent.

DURING THE WINTER: Murres spend the winter at sea in the cold waters off the North Atlantic and North Pacific coasts, as well as the west coast of Greenland.

FEATHERED FACT: Each murre egg has a special pattern that is different from every other egg. A murre memorizes the pattern on its egg so that it can recognize it among a crowd of eggs.

Arctic Tern
Inuktitut Name: *Imiqqutailaq*

↑ Length: 33–36 cm
↓ Wingspan: 76–85 cm

This graceful, grey-and-white seabird has long, slim wings, a black cap, and a long, forked tail. Its legs, webbed feet, and dagger-sharp bill are all coloured a brilliant red. The male and female look alike, and pairs stay together for life.

Where to Look: Arctic terns nest in big, noisy colonies on open tundra along Arctic shores. Look for these "sea swallows," as they are sometimes called, as they hover and dive in busy groups above the waves. Watch how the sun shines through their see-through wing feathers as they fly.

What They Eat: Arctic terns tuck their wings and dive like darts to catch fish and small marine critters just beneath the ocean's surface. This is called "plunge-diving."

Listen For: Terns make a sharp *"Kek! Kek! Kek!"* or a piercing, *"Kee-yarr"* call.

Nest: A tern's nest is a small dent scraped into the ground that is sometimes lined with bits of grass or lichen. Terns nest close together, and when a predator comes near the colony, terns form an angry mob that dives, pecks, and cries at the intruder until it runs away!

Egg: A tern can lay 1 to 2 speckled, olive-coloured eggs, but most often it lays 2. Eggs are laid right out in the open, but they have camouflage colours that make them very hard to see.

Chick: The tawny and black-speckled chicks hatch after 3 weeks and are round, fluffy, and almost invisible when they are standing still, because their feathers blend in so well with their surroundings. Both parents help to feed them fish and other ocean critters until they can fly.

During the Winter: Arctic terns make the longest journeys of any bird on earth. They fly all the way from the Antarctic to the Arctic in the spring, and return to the Antarctic as the northern summer fades.

A Note about Nests: Finding a bird's nest is like finding a secret treasure. Nests come in many different shapes and sizes, and eggs can have bright colours and interesting patterns. If you find a nest, stay just a moment to take a quiet peek. Ask yourself: *What is it made of, and how is it hidden?* Be careful not to touch the eggs, or to stay so long that the parent bird becomes worried! Without a parent to cover them, uncovered eggs will cool quickly, and can also be spotted by gulls or foxes.

FEATHERED FACT: When a tern colony
is startled, all the birds fly up out of the
colony at once, circle around in the sky,
and then settle back on the ground all
together. This is called "dreading."

Red Phalarope
Inuktitut Name: *Saurraq*

↑ Length: 18–20 cm
↓ Wingspan: 40–45 cm

The female red phalarope is slightly bigger than the male. Her dark cap, white cheeks, and bright, rusty chest and belly make her much more colourful than the male. Phalaropes have long necks, short, grey legs, lobed toes, and yellow bills tipped with black.

Where to Look: Red phalaropes nest in wet tundra along Arctic shores. They like to nest close to Arctic terns, because terns chase away the predators that come looking for eggs!

What They Eat: Phalaropes eat insects and their larvae, snails, and crustaceans, picking up food as they wade along the shore. They also spin on the surface of the water in fast, tight circles, making whirlpools that pull food up to the surface where their bills are waiting!

Listen For: The phalarope's call can be a high *"Pseet!,"* a long *"Sw-eet!,"* or a whistling *"Wit!"*

Nest: Phalaropes make a small hollow lined with moss, grass, or lichen that is often hidden in the grass close to water.

Egg: A phalarope lays 4 olive-coloured eggs freckled with brown. After laying her eggs, the female phalarope leaves the male behind to care for the eggs and chicks all on his own.

Chick: The downy, cinnamon-coloured chicks hatch after 18 to 24 days and can leave the nest on their first day out of the egg to hunt for food!

During the Winter: Phalaropes change into grey-and-white feathers for the winter and fly south to the deep, warm waters of the southern Atlantic ocean, off the coasts of South America and southwest Africa.

FEATHERED FACT: As they migrate, phalaropes have been known to gather in flocks around grey whales and bowhead whales, feeding on the crustaceans that the whales stir up from the mud as they are feeding.

Common Eider

↑ Length: 50–71 cm
↓ Wingspan: 80–110 cm

This large sea duck has thick feathers that keep it warm in icy seas. The male and female look quite different from each other, especially in the spring. The female has finely striped grey and cinnamon-coloured feathers, while the male is much more colourful. He has a black cap, a sloping bill, and green patches on his head. His breast is bright white, while his belly and tail are black. Both the male and the female have large, bluish-grey, webbed feet.

WHERE TO LOOK: Common eiders nest together along Arctic coasts. They like to nest on ocean islands where it is harder for predators, like foxes and polar bears, to reach them.

WHAT THEY EAT: Eiders gather together in shallow water to dive for mussels and crustaceans that live on the ocean floor. Their wings and large feet help them swim down to the ocean bottom.

LISTEN FOR: Male eiders make a ghost-like *"Ah-WOO-oo!"* call as they float together on the ocean, and the female eider clucks as she guards her chicks. Eiders also make a low, grunting *"Kor-korr-korr"* call when alarmed.

NEST: To build their nests, eiders scrape a hollow into the ground and line it with moss or seaweed, as well as soft, warm down that the female plucks from her own breast. As she sits on her nest, the female's feathers blend in so perfectly with the tundra that she can hardly be seen.

EGG: An eider lays 2 to 8 large, pale-green eggs.

CHICK: The downy, dusty-brown ducklings hatch after about 25 days. Not long after their feathers dry, the female leads them in a small parade down to the ocean.

DURING THE WINTER: Common eiders spend the winter close to the ice edge in cold, northern seas. Some eiders even spend the winter in openings in the sea ice called "polynyas."

FEATHERED FACT: At sea, ducklings float together in a *crèche* (the French word for cradle) that can contain over a hundred ducklings! Female eiders that haven't had their own young help to care for the ducklings in this floating daycare.

Long-tailed Duck

Inuktitut Name: *Acgiarjuk*

↕ Length: 39–47 cm
↕ Wingspan: 65–82 cm

This talkative sea duck is named for the long, black tail feathers that the male waves in the air behind him. Male long-tailed ducks change their feathers several times a year, trading bright winter feathers for less striking summer feathers. Long-tailed ducks have dark backs and wings, pale bellies, short, broad bills, and dark cheek patches. Their legs and large, webbed feet are a bluish-grey colour.

Where to Look: Long-tailed ducks nest together near tundra lakes and ponds, and along Arctic coasts. They like to nest close to Arctic terns, as terns chase away the predators that come near.

What They Eat: Long-tailed ducks are one of the deepest-diving ducks, and can dive down to 60 metres below the surface! They dive for insect larvae, molluscs, fish, and crustaceans.

Listen For: Females make a short, barking call when alarmed, while the males make a loud, yodelling "*Upup-ow-oowelep*" call. Long-tailed ducks are musical birds that love to call.

Nest: Long-tailed ducks nest in a hollow scraped into the ground and lined with tundra leaves and the birds' own soft down. Nests are usually located not far from fresh water, on peninsulas and islands.

Egg: Long-tailed ducks lay 6 to 9 cream to light-green eggs that are cared for by the female.

Chick: The downy brown ducklings hatch after 25 to 28 days and leave the nest soon after they dry to hunt for food.

During the Winter: Long-tailed ducks seek sheltered bays along rocky northern ocean coasts and large lakes to pass the winter.

FEATHERED FACT: Long-tailed ducks like to sneak their eggs into the nests of other long-tailed ducks, so some ducks end up sitting on eggs and raising chicks that are not their own!

TUNDRA SWAN

INUKTITUT NAME: *QUGJUK*

↑ LENGTH: 120–150 cm
↓ WINGSPAN: 168–211 cm

The tundra swan is snowy white, except for its black bill, legs, and feet. It has a long, straight neck, and some swans have a bright yellow patch, called a "lore spot," between the base of their bill and their eye. The male and female look alike, and pairs stay together for life.

WHERE TO LOOK: Tundra swans nest near tundra lakes, ponds, and marshy areas. Watch as they race across the water into the wind, lifting up into the sky with their long, graceful wings.

WHAT THEY EAT: Swans nibble on plants that grow in shallow water. Their long necks help them reach underwater to pull up tender roots, seeds, and leaves. They also eat some insects and snails.

LISTEN FOR: Tundra swans make a clear, sad *"Klooo"* song, along with a high, yodelling *"Whoo-hoo"* call mixed with yelps and barks and a loud, honking call. A musical murmuring can be heard as they rest together in a flock.

NEST: A tundra swan's nest is a large, raised bowl made of tundra plants and lined with a bit of down. Both the male and female help make the nest, building it near a lake or pond on a high spot where swans can see far into the distance to watch for predators. Tundra swan pairs nest alone, protecting a large area around their nest.

EGG: Swans lay 3 to 5 cream-coloured eggs.

CHICK: The downy, grey chicks, called "cygnets," hatch after about 32 days and can leave the nest within a day to swim and search for food with their parents.

DURING THE WINTER: Tundra swans head south to spend the winter in large flocks on shallow bays along the Atlantic and Pacific coasts of North America and on large inland lakes and rivers.

FEATHERED FACT: Tundra swans used to be called "whistling swans" because of the sound that their long, white wings make when they fly. Tundra swans have huge wings that stretch out over 2 metres!

GYRFALCON
INUKTITUT NAME: *Kiggaviarjuk*

 LENGTH: 48–64 cm
WINGSPAN: 110–130 cm

This fast, powerful hunter has dark eyes ringed with gold, broad, pointed wings, and a long, wide tail. A faint "moustache" can be seen on either side of its sharp, hooked beak, and its yellow feet are tipped with talons. Although they can be pure white or very dark in colour, most gyrfalcons are grey. The male and female look alike, but the female is much larger than the male.

WHERE TO LOOK: These stealthy hunters prefer bare, open tundra, high mountains, ocean coasts, and cliffs. They like to perch on rocks and bathe in cold, rushing Arctic streams.

WHAT THEY EAT: Gyrfalcons fly low and surprise their prey, chase birds over long distances to tire them out, and even strike birds in the air. They mainly eat ptarmigans, but also hunt geese, ducks, other birds, Arctic hares, and small mammals.

LISTEN FOR: The gyrfalcon cries a sharp *"KYHa! KYHa! KYHa!"* call, or a *"Kak kak kak!"* when alarmed.

NEST: Gyrfalcons don't build their own nests but use the old nests of other birds, such as ravens. They like to nest on cliff ledges, and the same nest site may be used by gyrfalcons for hundreds, even thousands, of years.

EGG: A gyrfalcon lays 2 to 7 creamy-white eggs freckled with reddish-brown spots.

CHICK: The downy, cream-coloured chicks hatch after 34 to 37 days and beg for food at the nest. Both parents care for the eggs and chicks.

DURING THE WINTER: Some gyrfalcons spend all year in the Arctic, while others migrate farther south. During the winter, gyrfalcons hunt for ptarmigans across the tundra, and fly out over the sea ice to hunt for seabirds.

FEATHERED FACT: The gyrfalcon is the world's largest falcon.

Snowy Owl
Inuktitut Name: *Ukpigjuaq*

↑ Length: 52–71 cm
↓ Wingspan: 130–150 cm

This pale, graceful owl has a round head, bright, golden eyes, and broad, white wings. Both its body and legs are thickly feathered, and its powerful feet are tipped with long, black talons. The males are either completely white, or are lightly marked with brown. The females are larger than the males, and have more brown markings on their feathers.

Where to Look: As the snow melts in the Arctic, watch for the strange spring dance of the snowy owl. He leaps into the air with a lemming in his beak, spreads his wings as he descends, and bows to the female in an effort to impress. Snowy owls can also be seen making short, low flights on their silent wings across the tundra.

What They Eat: Snowy owls mainly eat lemmings, but they also hunt for ptarmigans, hares, weasels, ducks, and geese. Special circles of feathers on the owl's face send the smallest sounds to its ears. They perch on rocks and turn their pale faces from side to side as they watch and listen for prey. The owl swallows its prey whole, and a lump of feathers, fur, and bones, called a "pellet," is spit out afterwards.

Listen For: The snowy owl's deep, raspy hoot can be heard for over 10 kilometres across the tundra. Snowy owls can also hiss, make harsh barking sounds, and snap their bills if they are threatened, but most of the time they are quiet.

Nest: To build her nest, the female snowy owl makes a shallow hollow by scraping away the dirt and pressing her belly into the earth. The nest is built on a high spot where the owl family can see out across the tundra. The male feeds the female as she sits on the nest.

Egg: A snowy owl lays 3 to 12 long, white, oval-shaped eggs.

Chick: The pale, downy owl chicks, called "owlets," hatch after 30 to 33 days. Owlets are fed lemmings and other prey by their parents until they can hunt on their own. The mother owl tears the prey into little bite-sized pieces for the owlets.

During the Winter: Some snowy owls stay in the Arctic all year round, hunting on the tundra and across the sea ice. When food is scarce, they will fly south of the Arctic, as far as the mid-United States.

FEATHERED FACT: Sometimes the entire owl family must move camp to find more lemmings. Before they can fly, owlets will walk along, following their parents. If they must cross a stream too deep to wade, the owlets can row across, using their fluffy wings like oars!

COMMON RAVEN

INUKTITUT NAME: *TULUGAQ*

↕ LENGTH: 33–36 cm
↕ WINGSPAN: 76–85 cm

This large, intelligent bird has glossy black feathers, a heavy, curved beak, and crafty, gleaming eyes. It has a wedge-shaped tail, slim wings with long, splayed feathers, and a tuft of shaggy feathers beneath its chin that looks like a beard. Raven pairs form strong bonds and stay together for life.

WHERE TO LOOK: Ravens soar over the tundra and along Arctic coasts, wheeling and playing on the wind. They hunch in their dark cloaks along telephone wires, and gargle and sing from the rooftops of tiny Arctic towns.

WHAT THEY EAT: Ravens eat everything—insects, eggs, garbage, carrion, seabird eggs and chicks, small mammals, fruit, fish, crustaceans, and seeds. Ravens break open mussel shells by dropping them on rocks and follow other animals to eat what they leave behind.

LISTEN FOR: Ravens make long, deep croaks; chortling, laughing calls; a raspy *"Kraaa!"*; and a variety of clicks and whistles. The language of ravens changes depending on where they live. Ravens in different parts of the world sing different songs and speak different words … what clever birds!

NEST: Ravens build a huge, messy stick nest lined with soft plants, animal hair, and found treasures like bits of cloth, rope, and plastic that is patched up and used year after year. With no trees in sight, Arctic ravens like to nest on cliffs, choosing sheltered stone ledges to build their nests. Look for piles of dropped sticks at the bottoms of cliffs—if you find one, look up, and you just might spot a raven's nest!

EGG: A raven lays 4 to 5 greenish-blue eggs patterned with brown speckles.

CHICK: Raven chicks hatch after 18 to 25 days. They are born naked with their eyes closed and only little tufts of grey down growing here and there on their bodies. Young ravens have white streaks in their beaks that fade as they grow older. Both parents help care for and feed the chicks.

DURING THE WINTER: Ravens stay in the Arctic all year round, tumbling and playing in the cold Arctic wind while people huddle, warm inside their homes.

FEATHERED FACT: Ravens can be found in almost every habitat in the northern half of the world, but they have a special place among Arctic birds. They are the birds most commonly seen near Arctic towns, even in the deep darkness of winter.

Rock Ptarmigan

Inuktitut Name: *Aqiggiq*

↑ Length: 34–36 cm
↓ Wingspan: 54–60 cm

This plump tundra bird has a small head with a delicate bill and feathered legs and feet. The male has a bright red comb above each eye and a pale white belly, while the female has a brown, mottled belly. Rock ptarmigans have three different sets of feathers that they can change with the season. The female's mix of brown, black, and white summer feathers blends in so perfectly with the tundra that she is almost invisible when standing still.

Where to Look: Rock ptarmigans spend the summer on high slopes and bare, rocky tundra.

What They Eat: Ptarmigans use their tiny bills to nibble on leaves, flower buds, birch buds and catkins, berries, twigs, seeds, and some insects.

Listen For: Rock ptarmigans make a startled "*Ka-ka-ka*" sound when frightened into flight. The male also makes a soft, snoring "*Krrrr-ah*" as he searches for a female to woo. Ptarmigans will also cluck and trill together while looking for food, as if in conversation.

Nest: Ptarmigans nest in a hollow lined with feathers, leaves, plant fluff, grass, or moss that is built in a sheltered spot on the open tundra.

Egg: Ptarmigans lay 8 to 10 cinnamon-coloured eggs speckled with chocolate-coloured spots.

Chick: The downy, tawny-and-brown chicks hatch after 20 to 24 days. Chicks eat both insects and tundra plants and are cared for by the female parent.

During the Winter: Rock ptarmigans spend all winter in the Arctic, changing into pure white feathers to blend in with the snow. They dig through snow to nibble on plants, and search for food in places where caribou and muskoxen have scraped the snow away. During the winter, male and female ptarmigans separate, forming all-male and all-female flocks.

FEATHERED FACT: Birds that stay in the Arctic all year long, such as ptarmigans and snowy owls, need to know how to dress for the winter. White feathers help birds move secretly through the snow, so that they can avoid predators or sneak up on their prey. Thick, downy feathers keep them snug and warm. Ptarmigans use their feathered feet like snowshoes as they run across the drifts, and dive deep into snowbanks to shelter from the cold.

RED-THROATED LOON

INUKTITUT NAME: *QAQSAUQ*

LENGTH: 53–69 cm
WINGSPAN: 106–116 cm

The red-throated loon is the world's smallest loon. It has a silvery head with dark red eyes, and a bright, rusty-red throat. Dark on its back and pale on its belly, it holds its slim bill raised up in the air, and has fine black-and-white pinstripes running down the back of its neck. Its legs and large, webbed feet are located far back on its body, making it awkward on land but an excellent diver. While other loons must run across the water in order to fly, red-throated loons can take flight directly from land. The male and female look alike, with the male being only slightly larger.

WHERE TO LOOK: Red-throated loons nest along the Arctic coast, in wetlands and on the shores of small tundra lakes and ponds. Look for the special shape that they make as they fly. Unlike other loons, their backs are humped and their necks droop low as they beat their wings across the sky.

WHAT THEY EAT: These underwater hunters dive for small fish, marine invertebrates, snails, and crustaceans, using their feet to push themselves deep into the water. Loons will fly long distances from their nests to hunt for food in the ocean or in larger lakes.

LISTEN FOR: Red-throated loons let out a wailing cry, or a goose-like *"Kak-kak-kak"* as they circle their nest ponds. Unlike other loons, the female calls as well as the male, and pairs like to sing together across their lake.

NEST: A red-throated loon's nest is either a muddy scrape at the edge of a lake or pond that is lined with moss or grass, or a nest built out of a pile of water plants in shallow water. The male and female build the nest together, placing it close to the water's edge, where they can slip quickly away.

EGG: Red-throated loons usually lay 2 olive-coloured eggs, marked with brown spots.

CHICK: Downy loon chicks hatch after 26 to 28 days and can swim within 1 day of hatching! Both parents help care for the young.

DURING THE WINTER: Red-throated loons spend the winter in sheltered spots along the Great Lakes, and along the coasts of southern North America and northern Mexico. During the winter, the loon's dark back becomes so speckled with white that it looks like a starry sky.

FEATHERED FACT: Most birds have very light, hollow bones that help them to fly, but the bones of loons are quite heavy. This allows loons to sink underwater and stay beneath the surface as they hunt.

Snow Bunting

Inuktitut Name: Qaulluqtaaq

↑ Length: 16–18 cm
↓ Wingspan: 32–38 cm

The snow bunting nests farther north than any other songbird. The male has a white head, a small, dark bill, and long wings with black wingtips and bright white wing patches. The female has a rusty, speckled head and brownish feathers on her back. The legs of both the male and female are dark grey.

Where to Look: As the snow melts, snow buntings hop along in small patches of open tundra. They perch on boulders and bounce along the ground, hunting for bugs and seeds. Watch for the white flash of the bunting's wing patches as it flies. Snow buntings get their name from the appearance of a snow flurry when a flock rises up and flies off in a hurry.

What They Eat: Snow buntings nibble on summer insects, sedge, and the seeds of tundra plants. Follow the male bunting as he flies back to the nest with a spider in his bill!

Listen For: Snow buntings make a musical "*Twee-turee-twee-turiwee*" call; a low, warbling "*Hudidi feet feet feew hudidi feet feet feew hudidi*"; a clear, rising whistle; and quick, buzzing calls. Males fly high and sing as they flutter down to the ground.

Nest: Snow buntings build a loosely knit cup of dried grass, moss, leaves, and roots, lined with soft fur, ptarmigan feathers, and fluffy plant down. They choose cool, shaded spots among stones to build their nests, and must line their nest with a thick layer of feathers to keep it warm. The female bunting builds the nest, and the male feeds her while she sits patiently on the eggs.

Egg: A snow bunting lays 2 to 8 eggs that can be pale turquoise to light grey or cream in colour and spotted with brown.

Chick: The downy, grey chicks hatch after only 12 to 13 days and are cared for by both parents on a steady diet of tasty insects.

During the Winter: Snow buntings spend the winter along shores and open places throughout southern Canada, the northern United States, and parts of Alaska.

FEATHERED FACT: Even while there is still snow on the ground and the temperature is well below zero, snow buntings are one of the first birds to arrive in the Arctic in the spring. The male buntings arrive first, and wait for over a month for the females to arrive.

FURTHER READING:

A Complete Guide to Arctic Wildlife by Richard Sale

Birds of Canada by David M. Bird, Editor

Common Birds of Nunavut by Mark L. Mallory

National Geographic Field Guide to the Birds of North America by Jon L. Dunn & Jonathan Alderfer

The Birder's Handbook: A Field Guide to the Natural History of North American Birds by Paul R. Ehrlich

The Sibley Guide to Birds by David Allen Sibley

ACKNOWLEDGEMENTS

Thanks to the natural history exhibits at the Canadian Museum of Nature and the Folk Museum in Skógar, Iceland, where I was able to observe some of the eggs and species that I had not yet seen in the field. Thanks also to Michael Male of Blue Earth Films for comments on his snowy owl footage, and to Justin, patient reviewer and aficionado of all things wild.

AUTHOR

Mia Pelletier grew up exploring the lakes and forests of the Canadian Shield. Drawn to shorelines and wild places, Mia studied ecology and lived in California and the Magdalen Islands before moving to Baffin Island, Nunavut, in 2010. In Nunavut, she works with Arctic seabirds, and with Inuit on the co-management of protected areas. Mia enjoys exploring the Arctic tundra and learning about the fascinating plants, animals, and people that call this region home.

ILLUSTRATOR

Danny Christopher has travelled all over Nunavut as an instructor for Nunavut Arctic College. He lives in Toronto with his wife and three children, who keep his life in a constant state of chaos.

Red Phalarope

Rock Ptarmigan

Raven

Tundra Swan

Gyrfalcon

Snow Bunting

Arctic Tern

Snowy Owl

Long-tailed Duck

Thick-billed Murre

Common Eider

Red-throated Loon